Put Beginning Readers on the Right Track with

ALL ABOARD READING™

The All Aboard Reading series is especially designed for beginning readers. Written by noted authors and illustrated in full color, these are books that children really *want* to read—books to excite their imagination, expand their interests, make them laugh, and support their feelings. With fiction and nonfiction stories that are high interest and curriculum-related, All Aboard Reading books offer something for every young reader. And with four different reading levels, the All Aboard Reading series lets you choose which books are most appropriate for your children and their growing abilities.

Picture Readers
Picture Readers have super-simple texts, with many nouns appearing as rebus pictures. At the end of each book are 24 flash cards—on one side is a rebus picture; on the other side is the written-out word.

Station Stop 1
Station Stop 1 books are best for children who have just begun to read. Simple words and big type make these early reading experiences more comfortable. Picture clues help children to figure out the words on the page. Lots of repetition throughout the text helps children to predict the next word or phrase—an essential step in developing word recognition.

Station Stop 2
Station Stop 2 books are written specifically for children who are reading with help. Short sentences make it easier for early readers to understand what they are reading. Simple plots and simple dialogue help children with reading comprehension.

Station Stop 3
Station Stop 3 books are perfect for children who are reading alone. With longer text and harder words, these books appeal to children who have mastered basic reading skills. More complex stories captivate children who are ready for more challenging books.

In addition to All Aboard Reading books, look for All Aboard Math Readers™ (fiction stories that teach math concepts children are learning in school); All Aboard Science Readers™ (nonfiction books that explore the most fascinating science topics in age-appropriate language); All Aboard Poetry Readers™ (funny, rhyming poems for readers of all levels); and All Aboard Mystery Readers™ (puzzling tales where children piece together evidence with the characters).

All Aboard for happy reading!

GROSSET & DUNLAP
Published by the Penguin Group
Penguin Group (USA) Inc., 375 Hudson Street, New York, New York 10014, USA
Penguin Group (Canada), 90 Eglinton Avenue East, Suite 700,
Toronto, Ontario M4P 2Y3, Canada
(a division of Pearson Penguin Canada Inc.)
Penguin Books Ltd., 80 Strand, London WC2R 0RL, England
Penguin Group Ireland, 25 St. Stephen's Green, Dublin 2, Ireland
(a division of Penguin Books Ltd.)
Penguin Group (Australia), 250 Camberwell Road, Camberwell, Victoria 3124, Australia
(a division of Pearson Australia Group Pty. Ltd.)
Penguin Books India Pvt. Ltd., 11 Community Centre, Panchsheel Park,
New Delhi—110 017, India
Penguin Group (NZ), 67 Apollo Drive, Rosedale, North Shore 0632, New Zealand
(a division of Pearson New Zealand Ltd.)
Penguin Books (South Africa) (Pty.) Ltd., 24 Sturdee Avenue,
Rosebank, Johannesburg 2196, South Africa

Penguin Books Ltd., Registered Offices:
80 Strand, London WC2R 0RL, England

Photo credits: cover: © Jeff Corwin, background photos: © Rob Tilley/Nature Picture Library,
© Jack Dykinga/Nature Picture Library; additional photos (clockwise from top right): © Philippe Clement/
Nature Picture Library, © George Grall/National Geographic/Getty Images, © Brand X Pictures/Brand X
Pictures/Getty Images, © David Kjaer/Nature Picture Library, © Dorling Kindersley/Geoff Brightling/
Staab Studios, © Brand X Pictures/Brand X Pictures/Getty Images, © Martin Harvey/Photographer's Choice/
Getty Images, © Jeff Foott/Discovery Channel Images/Getty Images; interior background:
© Niall Benvie/Nature Picture Library; page 3 (clockwise from center): © Linda Lewis/Botanica/
Getty Images, © Premaphotos/Nature Picture Library, © Dorling Kindersley/Geoff Brightling/Staab Studios,
© William Vann/Edupic Graphical Resource, © David Kjaer/Nature Picture Library; border (pages 4-48):
© Jack Dykinga/Nature Picture Library; page 4: © Jeff Corwin; page 5: (top) © Altrendo Nature/Altrendo/
Getty Images, (bottom) © Rolf Nussbaumer/Nature Picture Library; page 6: © Buddy Mays/Taxi/
Getty Images; page 7: © Premaphotos/Nature Picture Library; page 8: © David Kjaer/Nature Picture
Library; page 9: (top) © Frank Greenaway/Dorling Kindersley/Getty Images, (middle) © Gerry Ellis/
Digital Vision/Getty Images, (bottom) © Barry Mansell/Nature Picture Library; page 11: © John Cancalosi/
Nature Picture Library; page 12: © Premaphotos/Nature Picture Library; page 13: © Jan Dauphin;
page 14: © John Cancalosi/Nature Picture Library; page 15: © Philippe Clement/Nature Picture Library;
page 17: © Pete Oxford/Nature Picture Library; page 18: © Geoff Brightling/Iconica/Getty Images;
page 19: © Wegner/ARCO/Nature Picture Library; page 20: © Rolf Nussbaumer/Nature Picture Library;
page 21: © John Cancalosi/Nature Picture Library; page 23: (left) © Hans Christoph Kappel/Nature Picture
Library, (right) © David Shale/Nature Picture Library; page 24: © Terry L McCormick/Flickr/Getty Images;
page 25: (top) © George Grall/National Geographic/Getty Images, (bottom) © Premaphotos/Nature Picture
Library; page 26: © William Vann/Edupic Graphical Resource; page 27: © Don Farrall/Digital Vision/
Getty Images; page 28: © Gary Vestal/Photographer's Choice/Getty Images; page 29: (top) © Hans Christoph
Kappel/Nature Picture Library, (bottom) © William Vann/Edupic Graphical Resource;
page 30: © Gerald J. Lenhard/Louisiana State Univ/Bugwood.org; page 31: © Robert F. Sisson,
Contributor/National Geographic/Getty Images; page 32: © Jim Rorabaugh/USFWS;
page 33: © Forrest Pangborn; page 34: © Stephen Buchmann; page 35: © Robert F. Sisson/National
Geographic/Getty Images; page 36: © Rolf Nussbaumer/Nature Picture Library; page 37: © Jan Dauphin;
page 38: © Dale Ward; page 39: © Alex Wild; page 40: © Clemson University/USDA Cooperative Extension
Slide Series/Bugwood.org; page 41: © Howard Ensign Evans/Colorado State University/Bugwood.org;
page 43: © Scott Bauer/USDA Agricultural Research Service/Bugwood.org; page 44: © Pete Oxford/
Nature Picture Library; page 45: © Robert Oelman/Photolibrary/Getty Images; page 46: (left)
© Joel Sartore/National Geographic/Getty Images, (right) © William Vann/Edupic Graphical Resource;
page 47: © William Vann/Edupic Graphical Resource; page 48: (top) © Rod Williams/
Nature Picture Library, (bottom) © Altrendo Nature/Altrendo/Getty Images

Library of Congress Control Number: 2009043966

ISBN 978-0-448-45178-7   10 9 8 7 6 5 4 3 2 1

JEFF CORWIN
CREEPY-CRAWLY CRITTERS

Grosset & Dunlap
An Imprint of Penguin Group (USA) Inc.

Hi, I'm Jeff Corwin and I'd like to take you to one of my favorite places on the planet—the deserts of the southwestern United States. I'm talking about the beautiful wilderness found in parts of Arizona, New Mexico, and southern California.

It may sound strange to say that I love

The Southwest is home to some fascinating animals, like this tarantula.

this part of the world so much. After all, it's one of the harshest places I've ever been. And, guys, you know I've been to some pretty wild places! The temperature here can reach 110 degrees Fahrenheit in the middle of the day. And at night it can be downright freezing! There's very little shade from the blinding sun here. And there's almost no water—except during the short rainy season, when powerful monsoons can cause flash floods.

So why do I love the Southwest so much? Because it's home to so many amazing creatures. There are reptiles like the Gila monster, mammals like the coyote, beautiful birds like the burrowing owl, and amphibians like the spadefoot toad.

But I think the most fascinating Southwest animals are the small, crawling creatures in this book. These guys have incredible ways of hunting and feeding, protecting themselves from predators, and reproducing.

You might think these critters are all insects, but they're not. They're called *arthropods*. An arthropod is an animal that doesn't have bones under its skin. Instead, it has a hard, outer shell called an *exoskeleton*. Also, an arthropod's body is divided into segments. There are four kinds of arthropods in this book. The spiders, scorpions, and vinegaroon are called *arachnids*. Arachnids are creatures with four pairs of legs,

BLACK WIDOW SPIDER

bodies that are divided into two segments, and no antennae. Then there are *centipedes* and *millipedes*. All the other animals are *insects*, arthropods whose bodies are divided into three segments.

Many of these arthropods have stingers or fangs—but that doesn't mean we should be afraid of them. We just have to treat them with respect.

So, let's head out into the desert and find these crawling creatures of the Southwest!

DESERT HAIRY SCORPION ◈◈◈◈◈◈◈◈◈◈◈◈◈◈◈◈◈◈◈◈◈◈◈ ◆

Hiding in the shadows under sun-scorched rocks is the desert hairy scorpion. When darkness comes and the air cools, this wonderful arachnid emerges for its nightly hunt. It scurries over rocks on four pairs of legs. It searches for food by squeezing its flattened body through crevices. It clutches its prey with two large, menacing pincers. And it uses the stinger at the end of its curved tail to inject its victims with a poisonous liquid called *venom*. The venom isn't strong enough to kill a human, but it's more than enough to kill insects!

Most scorpions grow to a length of two to four inches, but the desert hairy scorpion can grow as long as six inches! That makes it the largest scorpion in the US. And the desert hairy doesn't just outgrow other scorpions. It outlives them, too. Most scorpions live between two and five years. But this guy can survive to the ripe old age of twenty-five!

DESERT HAIRY SCORPIONS

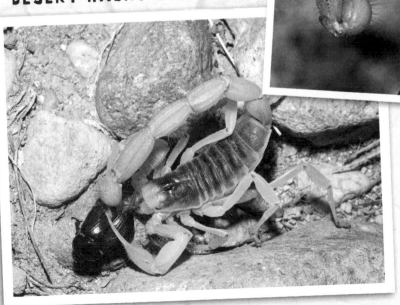

Like most scorpions, the desert hairy scorpion is *nocturnal*. That means it's most active at night. In fact, most desert dwellers are like this. During the day they hide under rocks, rest in the shade, or burrow underground to avoid the heat. At night they come out in search of food. The scorpion's body and legs are covered with hairs that it uses to feel vibrations from moving prey. The desert hairy eats all kinds of insects. But at six inches, it's large enough to prey on lizards and small snakes, too!

The desert hairy scorpion really shines at night. And when I say this guy shines, I mean it! If I want to find scorpions in the desert, I go out at night with a special lamp that gives off ultraviolet light. When the ultraviolet light hits the scorpion, an amazing thing happens. It glows in the dark! Believe me, guys, the sight of a scorpion glowing in the dark in the middle of the desert night is fantastic! Scientists call this *fluorescence*, although they're not sure why scorpions do this. For me, it's just another shining example of why I love the Southwest!

SCORPION UNDER ULTRAVIOLET LIGHT

GIANT VINEGAROON

To look at it, you might
think this arachnid just
stepped out of a horror movie!
Like a scorpion, it's armed
with two powerful pincers
to capture its prey. Its two-
inch-long body is covered
with a dark exoskeleton
that looks like armor.
Plus, it has a whiplike tail on its behind.
That's why its nickname is "whip scorpion."

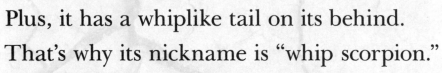

As scary as the vinegaroon looks,
it doesn't have a stinger or venom like a
scorpion. But that doesn't mean it can't
defend itself. When a predator attacks, this
guy has a trick up its sleeve. Well, in its
rear end, anyway.

If a hungry animal gets too close,
the vinegaroon points its backside at its

attacker. Then it shoots a mist of acid from two glands in its rear end. This is the same acid that's found in vinegar, which is why this arachnid is called a vinegaroon. But the acid is much stronger than vinegar. In fact, it's the strongest acid you'll find in *any* living creature. Spraying the predator with a face full of acid gives the vinegaroon a chance to escape. Hmmm . . . I wonder if I could train a vinegaroon to squirt my French fries!?

GIANT VINEGAROON PROTECTING ITSELF

BLACK WIDOW

The female black widow has a shiny black or dark brown body that measures about one-half to three-quarters of an inch long. There's no mistaking this beautiful arachnid. Look on her underside and you'll clearly see a bright red mark shaped like an hourglass.

Like most spiders, the black widow does something no other kind of animal can. It spins a web. Guys, spiderwebs are

BLACK WIDOW SPIDER

incredible! Spiders build them using a liquid that they make with special glands in their rear ends. When the liquid touches air, it turns into a thread of silk.

This stuff is unbelievable! A strand of spider's silk is as strong as a strand of steel. And talk about light! A thread of silk long enough to stretch around the world would weigh less than a pound. Not only that, but spiders produce different kinds of silk for different jobs. The strongest silk is used to build the "frame" of the web. Then there's sticky silk for catching prey. This is used on the inside of the web. Spiders also use this fantastic material to spin cocoons that hold their eggs or captured insects.

Can you guess why this spider is called a black widow? It's because the female does a very odd thing after mating. She kills the male . . . and eats him! Now, there are many kinds of black widow spiders around the world, and only some kill and devour their mates. In fact, the black widows of the Southwest don't seem to do this. Hmm . . . if I were a male black widow, I think I'd want to live in the Southwest!

After the female has mated, she lays about 300 eggs in her web and wraps them in a cocoon. When the black widow spiderlings hatch and leave home, they travel in a surprising way. They fly! No, they don't have wings. Small spiders fly by climbing to where there's some wind, like at the tip of a branch. Then they let out a long thread of silk. The silk catches the wind like the tail of a kite and the thread lifts the spider into the air like a hot air balloon! That's why they call it "ballooning"! The spider rides the wind until the breeze dies and it lands on the ground or in a bush. Boy, is there anything spiders can't do with their silk?

BLACK WIDOW WITH
EGG SACS

WESTERN DESERT TARANTULA

Check out one of my all-time favorite creatures: the western desert tarantula. This giant spider can grow to have a leg span of up to four inches! It has a bulky body and thick legs covered with hair. Like the scorpion, it uses its hair to feel for vibrations coming from predators and prey.

Arachnids have no teeth. That means the tarantula doesn't bite and chew its food the way other animals do. Instead, the western desert tarantula injects its prey

with venom. Not only does the poison paralyze its victim, but the venom turns the insides of the insect into liquid. When the venom has done its job, the tarantula sucks the liquid out of its victim like it's drinking a milkshake. That may sound gross to some people, but I think it's pretty cool!

In fact, I think the tarantula is an all-around amazing creature. But it's been given a bad rap. On TV or in the movies, this arachnid is always shown as a deadly creature that attacks people. But that's not the case at all. It's true that the tarantula is venomous, but tarantula venom isn't deadly to humans. If one does bite a person, it's probably because it's not being handled properly and feels threatened. It's

BROWN TARANTULA IN DEFENSE POSE

not attacking—it's just trying to protect itself.

The tarantula has another fascinating way of protecting itself. When an animal like a bird, coyote, or fox attacks, the tarantula uses its legs to flick hair from its abdomen. The hairs have tiny barbs, so they stick in the skin, eyes, and nose of the predator. They can cause enough stinging and itching to make the hungry attacker look for a meal elsewhere. I guess if it means not being eaten, the tarantula would gladly go a little bald!

TRAP-DOOR SPIDER ◇◇◇◇◇◇◇ ◆

When it comes to building a new home, trap-door spiders are just like humans. The three most important things are location, location, and location! To humans, that might mean a quiet street with no traffic. But to a trap-door spider, the perfect location has lots of traffic—insect traffic, that is. After all, you don't have to go hunting when your prey comes to you!

The trap-door spider builds its home by digging a tunnel-like hole. It makes the walls with a mixture of saliva and dirt, and lines the tunnel with its silk. Next it builds the trapdoor out of silk and dirt. When the trapdoor is closed, it keeps out predators. The door even swings open and shut on a hinge made of silk!

Once the spider's home is finished, the proud owner closes the trapdoor and waits inside. With the door shut, the spider's home is perfectly hidden. When an insect comes crawling along, sensitive hairs on the spider's legs and body sense the movement. It opens the trapdoor and bursts from its lair! In a split second, the insect is caught and pulled underground, where it becomes the spider's dinner. It's like having a pizza delivered to your front door!

CLOSED TRAPDOOR

TRAP-DOOR SPIDER EXITING ITS HOME

GIANT DESERT CENTIPEDE ◆

Now, guys, you know me. I study and work with alligators, crocodiles, venomous snakes, and big, hairy spiders—and I find them all fascinating! But this next creature gives even me the willies! It's the giant desert centipede. Maybe it's because this creature can grow up to eight inches long and moves faster than most crawling arthropods. Maybe it's because it has so many long legs—not a hundred legs, but it still has dozens! Or maybe it's because it has venomous fangs for hunting. Whatever it is, this guy gives me the creeps!

Of course, all those things also make this fellow a fantastic hunter.

GIANT REDHEADED CENTIPEDE

Like many desert crawlies, the centipede
is nocturnal and hunts at night. It uses its
speed to catch insects and other arthropods.
Its flat body also lets it squeeze between
rocks in search of prey. Large centipedes
even prey on lizards and small rodents!
When it finds its meal, the centipede grabs
its victim with its long rear legs. Then it
injects venom into its captive with
its fangs. It may creep me out,
but I have to admit—it's one
amazing animal!

MILLIPEDE

See that creature winding its way over the desert floor like a tiny, reddish brown train? That's a millipede, and it's searching for a meal of dead leaves. This guy's body isn't flat, like a centipede's. It's rounder, like a tube. The millipede's long, winding body is divided into many segments, and each segment has four legs. Like the centipede, the millipede doesn't have as

MILLIPEDE

many legs as you might guess from its name. *Milli-* means "thousand." The millipede has a lot of legs, but not *that* many!

The millipede's hard, shiny exoskeleton protects it from drying out in the heat. It also protects the creature from hungry predators. The millipede will even roll itself into a tight coil for added safety. And if that's not enough, it has one more trick. Each side of a millipede's body is lined with tiny holes. When attacked, the millipede releases a liquid from the holes. The liquid smells and tastes terrible. After getting a whiff of that awful smell, most predators look for something else to eat!

GIANT SWALLOWTAIL BUTTERFLY

The Southwest is home to many kinds of butterflies, including the giant swallowtail—the largest butterfly in the US. When it is fully grown, this magnificent insect has a wingspan of at least four inches. Its black wings are decorated with brilliant yellow spots and stripes.

Like most insects, the swallowtail starts out life as an *egg*. When it hatches, it's

GIANT SWALLOWTAIL BUTTERFLY

called a *larva*. The larva then becomes a *pupa*. Finally, the pupa transforms into an *adult*. The swallowtail looks very different in each stage. You wouldn't guess they were the same creature. This change is called *metamorphosis*, and it's one of the most amazing life cycles of any creature on the planet.

SWALLOWTAIL EGG

SWALLOWTAIL CATERPILLAR

You may have seen butterfly larva before. They're called caterpillars! And they come in a fantastic variety of colors and shapes. But, to tell you the truth, the swallowtail caterpillar is downright weird! It's covered in patches of brown, gray, and white, and

SWALLOWTAIL SHOWING
ITS OSMETERIUM

has kind of a bumpy shape. In fact, it looks a lot like a piece of bird dropping.

You might not think it's a good thing to look like animal poop. But here's the thing. When you look like poop, other animals don't think you're a caterpillar. And if they don't think you're a caterpillar, they won't eat you! So it's not so bad!

If a predator *does* see through the swallowtail caterpillar's camouflage, the insect has a backup plan. When the caterpillar is attacked, a special organ appears from inside its body, just behind its head. It's called the *osmeterium*. When it's out, it looks like the caterpillar has bright orange horns or antennae. But more importantly, the osmeterium gives off a foul-smelling mix of chemicals that sends the predator packing.

When the caterpillar is grown, it attaches its rear end to a small branch and wraps itself in a cocoon. Inside the cocoon, the larva becomes a pupa. In the spring, the cocoon opens and the adult swallowtail butterfly emerges. In time, the butterfly will lay its own eggs and the amazing life cycle will start all over again.

SWALLOWTAIL COCOON

PINACATE BEETLE

The little pinacate looks like an ordinary black beetle, but if you're a predator, watch out! If you get too close to it, the beetle stands on its head and sticks its rear end in the air like it's doing a handstand. That's why one of the pinacate's nicknames is "clown beetle." So how does this clownish behavior protect the pinacate? Its other nickname—stinkbug—is a clue. When a predator attacks, the pinacate shoots an awful smelling black liquid from its raised rear end! The stink is enough to make most predators look for a meal somewhere else.

PINACATE BEETLE
DEFENDING ITSELF

The Cochiti natives of the Southwest tell a story about why the beetle hides its head. When the world was still very young, a pinacate beetle was

given a bag full of stars to place in the heavens. But the beetle was careless and spilled the twinkling lights across the sky. The pinacate was embarrassed about making such a mess. That's why, to this day, he hides his face in the sand when you meet him. And the stars the beetle spilled? They are the faint band of light stretching across the night sky that we call the Milky Way—or so the story goes.

CARPENTER BEE

The deserts of the Southwest are home to many kinds of bees. But unlike honeybees, which live in nests with lots of other bees, many desert bees live alone. Desert bees include the world's smallest bee—a tiny insect known as the *Perdita minima*, which is less than a tenth of an inch long. They also include one of the biggest, the carpenter bee, which can grow to be an inch and a half in length.

PERDITA MINIMA ON THE HEAD OF A CARPENTER BEE

The carpenter bee may not build its home with a hammer and a saw, but it does use wood. The bee has strong jaws—strong

enough to dig into a tree or the woody branch of a plant. Once the carpenter has dug out a hole for its nest, it mixes together some chewed up wood and saliva. It uses this building material to create small compartments or cells inside the nest. The bee then places a supply of food in each cell. The food is a paste made of pollen and nectar. Finally, it lays a single egg in each cell, seals the cells, and flies away. When the eggs hatch, the larvae feed on the paste until they become adult bees. Then they chew their way out of their cells and head out on their own.

RED HARVESTER ANT ⬦⬦⬦ ◆

It's hard to imagine, but there are great "cities" hidden beneath the deserts of the Southwest. Thousands and thousands of desert dwellers make their homes in underground tunnels and chambers. They raise their young, work, and eat beneath the surface. Of course, the creatures I'm talking about are ants!

One of the most common ants in the Southwest is the red harvester. This reddish brown insect grows to about half an inch in length. Red harvester ants are *social* insects, like termites and honeybees. That means

RED HARVESTER ANT

they live together in *colonies*.

Each ant in the colony has a job to do. Harvester ant scouts search for seeds—the

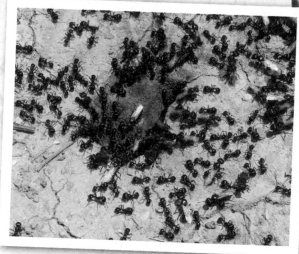

RED HARVESTER ANT COLONY

colony's favorite food. The scout leaves the nest in the morning to explore the desert while it's still cool. Once the scout finds some seeds, it returns home. On the return trip, the scout leaves a chemical trail between its find and the nest.

Now it's time for the worker ants to do their jobs. They follow the chemical trail to the new food and carry the seeds back to the nest in their pincerlike jaws. The ants store their harvest in chambers belowground, where there's enough food

RED HARVESTER ANT CARRYING A PEBBLE

for the whole colony.

The ant with the most important job in the colony is the queen. Hers is a task no other ant can do—laying eggs. A queen can live for up to twenty years. In that time, she will lay thousands and thousands of eggs! Usually, those eggs produce a female ant. That's why all the ants in a colony are sisters! But every year, a few ants called *alates* are born.

Alates are special ants with wings. They can be either female *or* male. These ants have a job to do, too. Their job is to fly away from the nest and mate. Once the female has mated, she's ready to start a new colony of her own. She finds a spot in the desert to her liking, burrows into the ground, and begins to lay eggs. She also sheds her wings. She is now a queen—and she'll soon have a large colony of her own.

ALATE

ANTLION

The antlion may not be a real lion, but if you're a tiny insect, it's still a deadly predator to be feared. The antlion looks harmless enough. It has a plump, round body, and grows to be about half an inch long. But it also has long, curved jaws that it uses to capture its prey.

The antlion has a surprising way of hunting. Look closely at the ground and you'll see small, funnel-shaped pits in the

ANTLION

sand. Antlions dig these holes and hide themselves at the bottom. When an insect like an ant stumbles into

ANTLION PITS

a pit, it gets stuck. As it tries to climb, the sand walls cave in. To make it even harder to escape, the antlion flicks sand at the ant from the bottom of the pit.

When the ant slips down to the bottom of the sandy trap, it slides right into the antlion's gaping jaws. The hunter then injects its prey with a venom that paralyzes the insect. The venom turns the insides of the ant into a liquid, and the antlion gulps down its meal like an ant-flavored juice box!

TERMITES

To many people, termites are pests because they eat wood. But in the deserts of the Southwest, this makes termites a very important insect. Why? Well, there are a lot of dead trees, shrubs, and cacti in the desert. There's a lot of animal dung, too. But the desert is also very dry. That means dead plants and dung don't rot the way they would in a forest. And if they don't rot, their nutrients don't go back into the ground to feed other plants.

That's where the termites come in. Termites eat the dead plants and animal dung. The nutrients in the wood and dung are then recycled back into the ground in the termites' droppings, or when the insects die. Termite dung breaks down quickly, so it doesn't build up like the dung of other animals would.

If all the termites disappeared, the desert would become a very different place. Before long, we'd be up to our eyeballs in dead wood and dung. Then, with no nutrients in the soil, plants would disappear. And without plants, animals would disappear. If it weren't for termites, I don't think the Southwest would be one of my favorite places!

TERMITES FEEDING ON DEAD WOOD

TARANTULA HAWK WASP

Do you see that big wasp scurrying over the rocks? That's a female tarantula hawk wasp, and she's searching for food. But she isn't looking for her next meal. She's looking for a tarantula spider to feed her offspring. The wasp uses her keen sense of smell to find a tarantula hiding in its underground burrow. When she finds one, she tricks it into thinking she's prey. The spider thinks lunch has arrived and emerges from its home . . . to a painful surprise!

Before the tarantula realizes what's happened,

TARANTULA HAWK WASP ATTACKING A TARANTULA

the wasp paralyzes the
big arachnid with her
sting. Then she drags
her prisoner back into
its burrow and lays a
single egg on it. The
wasp seals the burrow

**TARANTULA HAWK
WASP**

with dirt and small rocks and flies off.

In three or four days, the wasp larva
hatches from the egg. Over the next few
months, it eats the spider its mother has
left for it. Then it spins itself a silk cocoon.
Inside the cocoon, the larva slowly changes.
Finally, in the spring, it emerges as an adult
tarantula hawk wasp. With its spectacular
blue-black body, long legs, and bright
orange wings, it's no wonder the adult
wasp was chosen as the state insect of
New Mexico.

VELVET ANT

You might be surprised to learn that the velvet ant isn't an ant at all. It's really a wasp. Its name comes from the fact that female velvet ants don't have wings, so they look a lot like ants. (In fact, ants and wasps are very closely related.) At least it's easy to understand why they're called *velvet* ants. These beautiful insects are covered with colorful, velvety hair.

There are several different kinds of velvet ants in the Southwest. One type is black with a brilliant yellowish white abdomen.

RED VELVET ANT

YELLOW VELVET ANT

Another is vivid red and black. A third is covered with long, white hairs.

WHITE VELVET ANT

You might think that bright colors would make it hard for an insect to hide from predators. But here's the thing—velvet ants are like many other brightly colored animals. It doesn't matter if they're easy to spot, because their bright colors send a warning to predators. The colors say, "Stop! If you attack me, you'll be sorry!"

If you think a velvet ant would make a good meal and ignore its warning colors, you'll feel one of the most painful stings of any insect. And believe me, once you've been stung by this gal, you're not going to try chowing down on a velvet ant again!

Now you know why I love the Southwest so much! It's full of such awesome animals! You can also see why it's important to protect

GILA MONSTER

a wild place like this. It may seem harsh and empty, but it's home to many different kinds of plants and animals. Some are found nowhere else in the world, and some are in danger of disappearing forever.

If you'd like to see these amazing animals up close, just make sure to do your research before you go. Find the best season to visit and the best time of day to go hiking. And take everything you need—including lots of respect for this magical place.